GREEK HEROES
AND MYTHICAL
BEASTS

DISCOVER THE MYTHS
AND LEGENDS OF ANCIENT GREECE

SELENE
NICOLAIDES

T0014811

CONTENTS

Many years ago, my father, George Nicolaides, was the curator of a small museum displaying artifacts from the ancient world. He was particularly fascinated by ancient Greece, and the museum owned many wonderful Greek objects. I was entranced by his stirring tales of gods and goddesses, of brave heroes, of vengeful spirits, and of terrifying monsters.

My father was strangely uneasy about one group of objects. They had been smuggled out of Greece in the nineteenth century and sold to the museum—a bust of the god Zeus, a coin showing the snake-haired monster Medusa, a statue of the baby Heracles strangling two serpents, and an exquisite gold earring depicting the hunting goddess Artemis.

A rumor had grown up about how the artifacts were somehow cursed, for the very day after they were put on display, the museum's keeper was killed in a lightning storm. Just a few years later, another curator was horribly injured when his own dogs savaged him.

My father told me these events were nothing but dreadful coincidences. However, when his own staff began to talk of how the bust of Zeus had inexplicably moved in the locked display case, my father was unnerved. When the same thing happened with the Artemis earring, he decided to remove the pieces from view. And that seemed to be the end of the matter, for I don't recall he ever spoke of it again.

When my father died, among his possessions was a curious box with a note attached: "Do not open—for Athens." I was intrigued and wondered if the "cursed" objects lay inside. However, as the daughter of a Greek scholar, the Pandora myth flashed across my mind. She was once given a box by the gods and told never to open it; when she did, all the troubles of the world poured out. And so although I knew it was silly superstition, I hid the unopened box away in my own attic.

Just over a year ago, I began to be troubled by loud knocks and scraping noises coming from the attic. I searched but could find no explanation. Then one night there was a great storm—in between crashes of thunder, the attic noises started up and were more insistent than ever. I was quite terrified.

In the morning, I climbed up to the attic and my eyes fell upon my father's box. The sealed lid had been forced open and inside I saw—with dread—the bust of Zeus gleaming in the half-light alongside the other pieces.

I immediately knew what I must do, and arranged for these treasures to be returned to their rightful home. Now housed in an Athens museum, they are shown in the pages of this book. I hope these mysterious objects will speak to you—as they did to me—of an ancient land rich in mystery and myth.

Selene Nicolaides,
London

LAND of GODS and HEROES

We owe much to the ancient Greeks for they were wonderful scientists, artists, and thinkers. They were also incredible storytellers. Greek myths tell of powerful gods and goddesses, of mysterious spirits, and of brave heroes who conquered terrifying monsters. These ancient tales are some of the greatest stories ever told and have inspired many famous works of art over the ages.

THE ANCIENT GREEK WORLD

The Greeks were one of the most advanced civilizations of ancient times. Their ideas in philosophy, politics, and science, and their achievements in the arts and sport have shaped the Western world. The Greeks were masterful storytellers–their stirring tales of powerful gods, daring heroes, and fabulous beasts live on today, as do the ruins of beautiful temples and buildings.

Some of the locations of the Greek mythical world, where heroes battled monsters and gods.

This gold vessel was found in a Mycenaean tomb.

In the Beginning

From roughly 2700 BC, the Minoans built a civilization that flourished on the island of Crete. Around 1400 BC, the Mycenaeans invaded Crete. Warriors and traders, they dominated the Greek world until around 1200 BC.

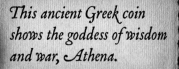

This ancient Greek coin shows the goddess of wisdom and war, Athena.

Classical Athens

The Dark Ages, a period from 1100 to 800 BC, was a time of decline. From the eighth century BC, many city-states–such as Sparta and Athens–began to form and gain power, and early Greek culture began to take shape. By the fifth century BC, Athens had become the most important city-state. It was a magnificent center for learning and the arts.

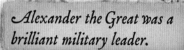

Alexander the Great was a brilliant military leader.

The Rise of Rome

King of the Greek kingdom of Macedonia from 336 BC, Alexander the Great invaded and conquered the Persian Empire. After he died, his empire was divided up into four Greek-ruled kingdoms. By 30 BC, however, all of Greece's colonies had fallen to the Romans.

Named after the Greek goddess Athena, the temple of Athena Nike stands on a rocky hill called the Acropolis in Athens.

GREEKS AT WAR

For the ancient Greeks, battle and bloodshed were part of everyday life. The most famous war in Greek mythology is the Trojan War, a conflict between the Greeks and the kingdom of Troy. Other myths tell of the Amazons, a legendary tribe of fearsome female warriors.

A Trojan warrior's shield.

RELIGION AND MYTHOLOGY

The ancient Greeks believed that powerful gods and goddesses ruled the world. The most important of these were the 12 Olympians who were said to inhabit a kingdom high up on Mount Olympus. However, there were many other gods, as well as demigods–children with one immortal and one mortal parent– and spirits. People worshiped the gods they found most useful. A Greek might have prayed to Zeus for rain, to Athena for success on the battlefield, or to Apollo for healing.

This ancient stone depicts the gods (from left): Hestia (sometimes considered an Olympian god, instead of Dionysus), Hermes, Aphrodite, Ares, Demeter, Hephaestus, Hera, Poseidon, Athena, Zeus, Artemis, and Apollo.

Tales of Gods and Mortals

Many Greek myths recount the adventures of gods and goddesses, and their dealings with humans. The gods are often shown as behaving like people–they fall in love and argue. Some tales recount how heroes overcome terrifying monsters, while other myths attempt to explain what lies behind the powerful forces of nature.

This table shows the 12 Olympian gods. Hestia and Hades were also considered important gods.

THE OLYMPIAN GODS

The 12 Olympian gods and goddesses are often portrayed in myths and in art with various symbols that help to identify them. This table shows some of their main symbols.

ZEUS
King of the gods, god of the sky
Symbol—thunderbolt

POSEIDON
God of the sea
Symbol—trident

APOLLO
God of the sun, music, and healing
Symbol—lyre

ATHENA
Goddess of wisdom and war
Symbol—owl

DIONYSUS
God of wine and celebration
Symbol—grapes

ARTEMIS
Goddess of hunting and the moon
Symbol—bow and arrow

ARES
God of war
Symbol—armor

HERA
Queen of the gods, goddess of marriage
Symbol—diadem

DEMETER
Goddess of nature, fertility, and the harvest
Symbol—wheat sheaf

APHRODITE
Goddess of love
Symbol—dove

HERMES
Messenger of the gods
Symbol—caduceus

HEPHAESTUS
God of fire
Symbol—hammer or ax

IN THE BEGINNING

The tales of ancient Greece go back to the dawn of time itself. In the beginning there was nothing but a vast and yawning emptiness: no Earth or moon, no day or night, and no gods or people. Yet out of this nothingness came a miracle— the appearance of the Earth and sky, the birth of the enormous Titans, and finally the creation of the mighty Olympian gods.

Mother Earth

The Greeks believed that at the beginning of time there was only a vast space called chaos. Out of this void came the Earth or Gaia, as well as Tartarus, a black pit beneath Earth. Uranus, the god of the sky, was born, followed by the sea and the mountains. Gaia married Uranus, and together they had many enormous children.

The Mighty Titans

The first of these children were the Titans, 12 immensely strong giants. Next came three Cyclopes, hideous one-eyed giants. Gaia then gave birth to three "hundred-handers". Horrified, Uranus banished some of these monstrous offspring deep within Tartarus. Gaia longed to see her children again. She gave the Titan Cronus a sickle made of adamant with which to attack his father. As Uranus's blood trickled down to Earth, the giants, the Furies, the nymphs, and Aphrodite—the goddess of love—were created.

The Birth of Venus by Sandro Botticelli. "Venus" was the Roman name for the goddess Aphrodite.

A Greek relief of Gaia.

A Roman floor mosaic showing Uranus and Gaia with some of their children.

Cronus, leader of the Titans, overthrew his father to take control of the universe.

WAR OF THE GODS AND TITANS

After defeating Uranus, Cronus became ruler of the universe. He married his sister Rhea, and she gave birth to the gods Hestia, Demeter, Hera, Hades, Poseidon, and Zeus. However, like his father before him, Cronus was afraid of being overthrown by his children, and so he swallowed each newborn god— all except the youngest, Zeus.

Cronus is fooled into thinking that a boulder wrapped in blankets is Zeus.

The Revenge of Zeus

When Zeus was born, Rhea hid the child away in a cave and handed Cronus a boulder wrapped in blankets instead. The king swallowed the rock and baby Zeus was raised by nymphs. When he was old enough, he vowed to take revenge on Cronus. Approaching him one day, Zeus punched his father in the stomach and made him vomit up the other gods one by one.

Rulers of the Universe

Stirred up with anger, the gods were led by Zeus in a war against the Titans. Helped by the hundred-handers and the Cyclopes, the gods were victorious and Cronus was banished from Earth. Zeus became god of the sky, Poseidon ruler of the sea, and Hades became lord of the dark underworld, Tartarus.

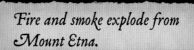

Fire and smoke explode from Mount Etna.

THE RAGE OF MOUNT ETNA

After the defeat of the Titans, Typhon, a hundred-headed dragon, rose up to challenge the mighty Zeus. However, the beast was soon defeated by the furious god and imprisoned beneath Mount Etna, a volcano on the island of Sicily. Legend has it that whenever the trapped beast writhes in rage, Mount Etna boils and spits out columns of fire.

The great battle between the Titans and the younger gods lasted for 10 years.

TYPHON

Known as the "father of all monsters," no beast was
feared more than the horrifying dragon Typhon.
This creature's numerous offspring included the
dreaded Sphinx and the gigantic Nemean Lion.

THE BIRTH OF MANKIND

Prometheus was a Titan who sided with Zeus in the great struggle against Cronus and the other Titans. Rewarded for his loyalty, he was given the task of creating mankind. Prometheus moulded shapes out of mud, designing people to walk upright so they could gaze up at the stars. Athena, the goddess of wisdom, breathed life into these human forms.

Prometheus's liver is ripped from his body by a mighty eagle.

The Gift of Fire

Prometheus sneaked up to Mount Olympus and stole sacred fire to give to man. Zeus was furious, for fire was for the gods alone. The Titan was chained to a cliff on Mount Caucasus. Every day, a great eagle appeared to peck out his liver. Prometheus's liver regrew each night, only to be ripped out again at sunrise. He endured this suffering for centuries, until finally the hero Heracles set him free.

In Greek mythology, Pandora was the first woman created on Earth.

Pandora's Box

To punish man for Prometheus's disobedience, Zeus ordered the other gods to make the first woman, Pandora. She was given a box and told never to open it. Overcome by curiosity, Pandora looked inside—out of the box flew all the ills of the world, and only hope remained inside.

Pandora's box contained all the evils of the world.

THE MIGHTY GODS

High up on the peaks of Mount Olympus lived immortal Zeus and the other Olympian gods. Although human in form and with many flaws, these powerful gods reigned supreme over the universe. The ancient Greeks worshiped a host of lesser gods too, while numerous nymphs and spirits had great powers over nature, human life, and death.

SUPREME GOD

Zeus was god of the sky, and king of the gods living on Mount Olympus. Often known as "Father Zeus", he ruled and watched over both gods and mortals. However, he was also the sender of rain, thunder, and lightning, and those who angered him were struck down by a thunderbolt or sent to the dark pit of suffering called Tartarus. Zeus was married to his sister, Hera.

This bust of Zeus seems to give off a strange energy. It is almost as if the god were living still...

George Nicolaides, 1962

Golden Eagle

Zeus's eagle served as his messenger and was his constant companion. Myth tells of how the eagle was once a much loved king called Periphas. When the king was honored as a god, Zeus grew jealous. In a rage, he was about to strike him down but Apollo transformed Periphas into an eagle and set him down at the side of Zeus. The god's other symbols were his thunderbolts and his scepter.

Hera was known for her jealousy and her marriage to Zeus was not a happy one.

QUEEN OF REVENGE

Even though Hera was the goddess of marriage, she was jealous of Zeus's many love affairs and constantly plotting revenge. One tale tells of how Zeus fell in love with a river nymph called Io. When Hera realized what was going on, Zeus transformed Io into a small cow. Hera saw through the trickery, however. Pretending to like the cow, she demanded it as a gift and then asked a hundred-eyed giant to watch over it. Zeus helped Io to escape but her freedom came at a price—Hera sent a horsefly to endlessly torment her, and she wandered the world without rest.

Mount Olympus was where the Olympian gods lived.

RULER OF THE SEA

Since Poseidon was king of the oceans, he had the power to stir the sea to a fury or to calm raging waters with a glance. Seafaring was an important part of Greek life, and sailors and fishermen prayed to Poseidon for protection. However, this Olympian was seen as a vengeful god too, and he was often referred to as the "Earth-shaker". When angered, Poseidon could punish mortals by causing devastating earthquakes.

In this Roman mosaic, Poseidon is shown riding across the ocean with his wife, Amphitrite.

RIDING THE WAVES

Poseidon is often shown with his wife Amphitrite riding across the ocean waves in a swift chariot pulled by golden seahorses. He carried a powerful trident to raise ocean waves and also to bring up new land from beneath the sea. Although Poseidon's official home was on Mount Olympus, he spent most of his time in his watery kingdom. He and Amphitrite had a son, Triton, who was half-man, half-fish.

This ancient Greek pitcher depicts Athena confronting Poseidon in the contest for Athens.

The Contest for Athens

Poseidon and Athena both wanted to control Athens, so each was asked to present the city with a gift. Poseidon struck the ground with his trident and a frothy spring burst forth–but the water was salty. Athena planted an olive tree, which granted the Athenians olives as well as oil. When the goddess was declared the winner, Poseidon stirred up a terrible sea storm that flooded Athens.

LORD OF THE UNDERWORLD

When the gods drew lots for the division of the universe, Hades received the gloomy realm of the underworld. This god is often shown wearing the cap of invisibility, made for him by the Cyclopes, and carrying a two-pronged fork. Cerberus, a ferocious three-headed hound, guarded the entrance to Hades's dark kingdom. All dead souls were permitted to enter but none could ever leave.

Hades and Persephone

One day, Hades ventured up to the world in his black chariot and came across Demeter's beautiful daughter, Persephone. He carried her off to be his queen, and because Demeter was full of grief, the Earth became barren. Zeus ordered that Persephone be returned to the land of the living, though only if she had eaten nothing in the underworld. Hades tricked Persephone into eating pomegranate seeds–she could go back to the world, but only if she returned to Hades for four months each year. During those months, Demeter mourned and the Earth was thrown into winter.

Hades seizes Persephone and carries her down to his underworld kingdom to become his queen.

LIFE AFTER DEATH

The Greeks believed that after death, their souls were guided down to the Styx river. As a boundary between the living and the dead, its waters were guarded by Charon. The dead were buried with a coin called an obolos to pay Charon to row them across the river. Three judges decided the fate of each soul. Those who had lived ordinary lives were sent to the joyless plains of Asphodel where they lived as pale ghosts of their former selves. The heroic were sent to the lovely Elysian Fields, while the wicked received terrible punishments in the dark pit of Tartarus.

Dead souls paid Charon to ferry them across the Styx with a silver coin called an obolos.

ORPHEUS AND EURYDICE

Orpheus was a wonderful musician, and it was said that even the birds and the beasts were enchanted by his beautiful music. When his beloved wife, Eurydice, died from a serpent bite, the heartbroken Orpheus vowed that he would journey down to the underworld to fetch her back.

Orpheus was said to be the best musician in the world—when he played his lyre, even animals were bewitched by his music.

Orpheus was inconsolable when Eurydice was bitten by a poisonous snake and he realized he might lose her forever.

Land of the Dead

Only dead souls were permitted to cross the Styx river. However, when Orpheus began to sing, Charon agreed to row the musician across the river. At the gate to the underworld stood the watchdog Cerberus. As the three-headed beast savagely bared its teeth, Orpheus began to play his lyre. Cerberus meekly lay down and Orpheus ventured into the icy darkness. All around him, he could hear the pitiful cries and wails of the shadowy dead.

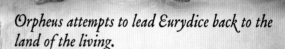

Orpheus attempts to lead Eurydice back to the land of the living.

LOVE BEYOND THE GRAVE

Finally Orpheus reached the cavern where Hades sat with Persephone. As he told of his heartbreak, Persephone began to weep. Hades agreed that Eurydice might leave on one condition: Orpheus must walk ahead of his wife and never once glance back. Overjoyed, Orpheus began the lonely walk back up to light. However, after many hours of total silence, he began to worry that Eurydice was not behind him after all–and couldn't resist turning round to check. She was there, but Orpheus had broken his promise: Eurydice fell away into the blackness and was lost to him forever.

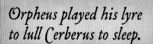

Orpheus played his lyre to lull Cerberus to sleep.

GODS OF LOVE AND WAR

Aphrodite was the beautiful goddess of love. Her name means "born from the foam" and myths tell of how she rose up from the surging sea when Uranus's blood dripped down to Earth. Zeus feared that rivalry among the gods over beautiful Aphrodite might lead to war, so he forced her to marry the god of fire, Hephaestus. This skilled god crafted magical weapons and exquisite jewelry from rock. However, he was ugly and lame, and Aphrodite was often unfaithful to him.

The famous Greek statue of Aphrodite known as the "Venus de Milo". Venus was the Roman name for Aphrodite.

This Greek vase shows Hephaestus riding on horseback.

ARES AND ATHENA

Ares was the hot-headed god of war and was unpopular. Usually shown with a helmet and sword, he represented the violence of battle. His half-sister, Athena, was goddess of war and wisdom— she was said to have sprung forth from Zeus's head fully armed. Athena was connected with military planning and victory, and it was to her that Greek soldiers prayed to for success. As the goddess of wisdom, Athena was often portrayed alongside her sacred bird, the owl.

Strong but merciless, Ares represented the brutality and chaos of war.

A coin from ancient Athens. Athena's symbol, the owl, still represents wisdom today.

In contrast to her half-brother Ares, Athena was associated with victory on the battlefield.

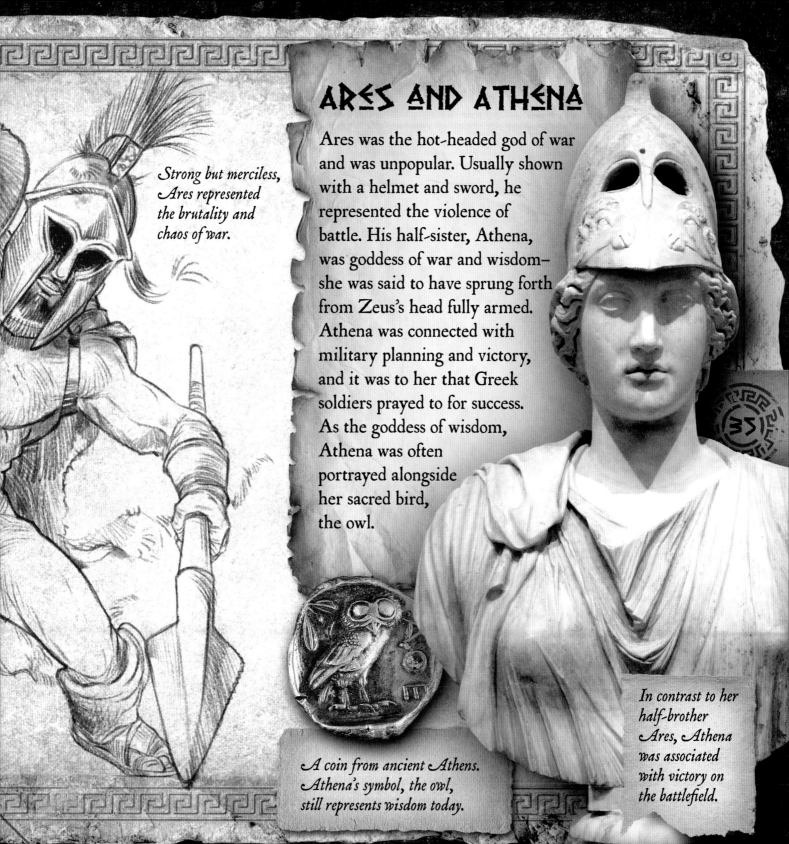

APOLLO AND ARTEMIS

Apollo was one of the most important gods of ancient Greece, and had many responsibilities. He was god of the sun, music, and healing, and of truth and prophecy. Apollo was often portrayed as a beautiful young man carrying a golden lyre or a quiver full of arrows. He was believed to speak to those seeking guidance through his oracle–a priestess called the Pythia–at his temple in Delphi.

Apollo's temple at Delphi was one of the most important sacred sites in ancient Greece.

Despite the delicate beauty of this earring depicting the hunting goddess Artemis, I cannot but think of her cruel treatment of Actaeon, and the savage manner of his death...

George Nicolaides, 1962

GODDESS OF THE HUNT

Apollo's twin sister was Artemis. As well as being the goddess of hunting, Artemis was also the goddess of the moon and of wild animals. She had the power to heal, but her arrows could also bring illness and death. Artemis was often depicted as a huntress. One myth tells of how a great hunter called Actaeon once glimpsed her bathing in a stream. She was so furious, she turned the man into a stag and he was savaged to death by his own hunting dogs.

The twin gods Apollo and Artemis were the children of Zeus and the Titan goddess Leto.

Actaeon is torn apart by his own hunting dogs.

HARVEST AND HOME

Demeter was the goddess of fertility and the harvest. She was worshiped during the Eleusinian Mysteries, secret celebrations held to mark the cycle of death and rebirth in nature. The Mysteries celebrated the return of Demeter's daughter, Persephone, back to Earth from the underworld and the start of spring. During these celebrations, Dionysus, the god of wine and celebrations, was also honored.

Home fires were kept alight to honor Hestia.

Demeter was often shown carrying fruits and grain.

Goddess of the Fireside

Hestia reigned over the home. Gentle and pure, she stood apart from the other quarrelling Olympians, and eventually gave up her place in Olympus for Dionysus.

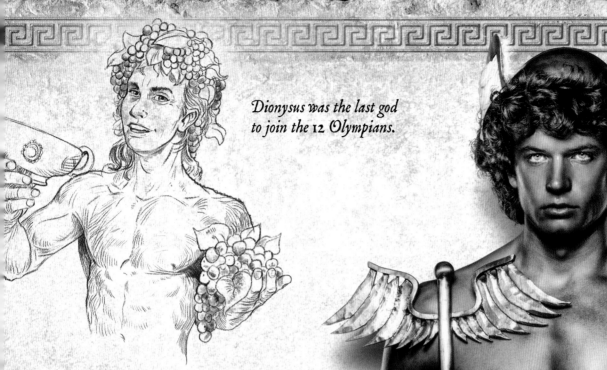

Dionysus was the last god to join the 12 Olympians.

The Pleasure-Loving God

Dionysus, the son of Zeus and a mortal called Semele, taught people how to make wine. He was often accompanied by his party-loving followers, goat-footed satyrs and nymphs called Maenads. Dionysus was unique among the Olympians in having a human parent. When Hera discovered that Zeus had been unfaithful, she tricked Semele into looking upon Zeus in his true god form and she perished in a blaze of fire. The unborn Dionysus was rescued and sewn into his father's thigh, and released on Mount Pramnos a few months later.

THE MESSENGER GOD

Hermes flew on winged sandals, carrying messages from gods to mortals, and showing dead souls the way to the underworld. He carried a winged staff called a caduceus.

Hermes's caduceus was a winged staff entwined with two snakes.

NYMPHS AND SPRITES

In addition to the important gods of Olympus, there were many other gods and spirits in Greek mythology. Four wind gods were linked to the changing seasons, while various gods watched over the rivers. Nymphs were beautiful female spirits associated with natural places. Oreads inhabited the mountains, while tree nymphs called dryads lived in the forests. Nereids were goddesses of the sea, and naiads tended freshwater streams and springs.

Pan was the god of wild places. He was half man, half goat.

Beautiful nymphs, such as this sea-dwelling nereid, watched over the natural world.

Magic and Sorcery

Some female spirits were believed to have great power over the lives of mortals. Hecate was the goddess of witchcraft and could see into the future. The beautiful goddess of magic, Circe, had a vast knowledge of magical potions and herbs, and was able to transform her enemies into wild beasts.

A Turkish stone bust of Hecate, the goddess of all things magical.

God of Arcadia

Pan was the goat-footed god of shepherds and flocks. He was said to come from Arcadia, a beautiful wilderness. Pan played musical pipes and enjoyed chasing after pretty nymphs. He once challenged Apollo to a musical duel, and all but King Midas agreed that Apollo was the better musician. Apollo punished King Midas for his poor hearing by giving him donkey ears!

Although she was very beautiful, Circe was in fact a sorceress renowned for her potions and spells.

ANCIENT CRAFTS

The ancient Greeks were skilled crafts people who made beautiful, intricate jewelry, and pots and vases that tell us much about their way of life. Often these everyday objects depicted scenes from mythology, or were dedicated to the gods.

ABOVE: This gold ring depicts Nike, the Greek goddess of victory.

ABOVE: An earring adorned with a pair of mythical griffin heads.

RIGHT: A pair of female-headed Sphinxes decorate this fine vase.

BELOW: A cup decorated with an image of Dionysus, the god of wine, aboard a ship.

LEFT: This mirror shows Aphrodite with winged figures representing Eros.

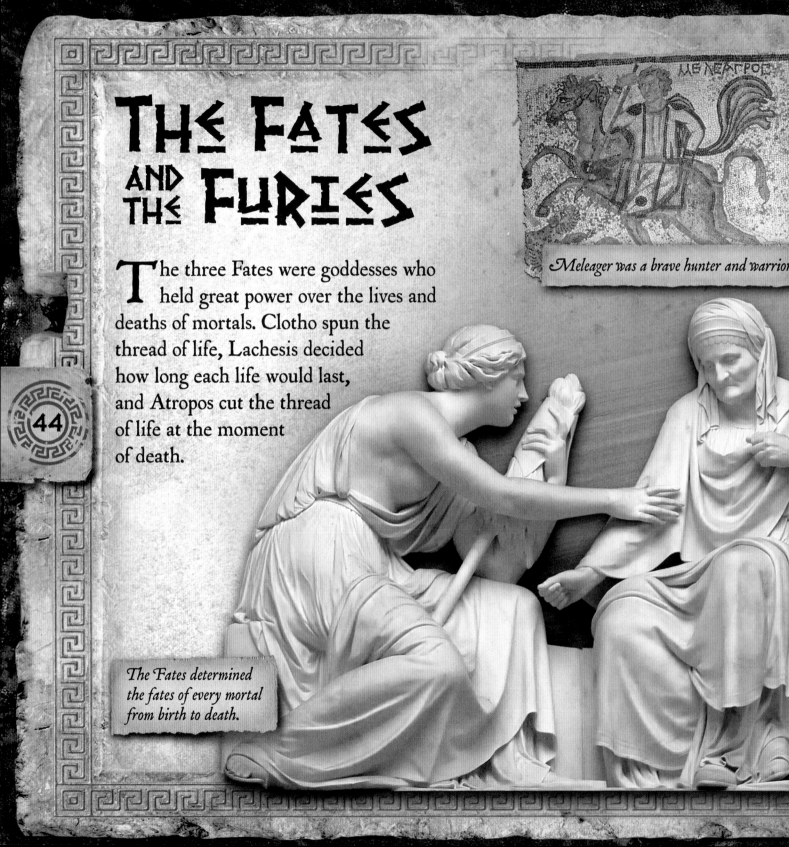

The Fates and the Furies

The three Fates were goddesses who held great power over the lives and deaths of mortals. Clotho spun the thread of life, Lachesis decided how long each life would last, and Atropos cut the thread of life at the moment of death.

МЕΛΕΑΓΡΟΣ

Meleager was a brave hunter and warrior

The Fates determined the fates of every mortal from birth to death.

Meleager's Fate

When Meleager was a baby, the three Fates appeared before his mother and told her that the child would live only as long as a brand burning upon the hearth remained unconsumed. Snatching the brand from the flames, she locked it away in a chest. Meleager grew up to be a valiant warrior, but when he killed his mother's brothers she took revenge. She cast the half-burnt brand back on the fire–and when it had turned to ash, Meleager dropped down dead.

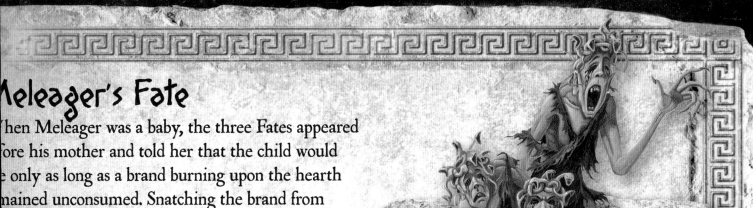

SISTERS OF REVENGE

The Furies were three monstrous sisters of the underworld with burning eyes and hair of writhing snakes. When they weren't torturing damned souls, it was their job to hunt down and punish wicked people–especially those guilty of murder. The sisters carried whips and cups of venom with which to torment wrongdoers. People sometimes referred to them as the "kindly ones" in the hope that this might protect them from the Furies' wrath.

MONSTERS AND MYTHICAL CREATURES

Ancient Greece teemed with a host of fabulous beasts and terrifying monsters. Golden sea horses galloped through the waves, while fierce centaurs prowled the woods. The dark gate of the underworld was guarded by the three-headed Cerberus, Scylla lurked in a sea cave waiting to crack the bones of passing sailors, and the horrifying Sphinx devoured all those unable to answer her riddle.

HALF MAN, HALF BEAST

Greek myths were full of strange creatures that combined both animal and human features. Most, such as the forest-dwelling centaurs, seemed more beast-like than human. Centaurs had the head, arms, and chest of a man, and a horse's body and legs. Although most were savage and unpredictable, some Centaurs–like the wise Chiron–were intelligent and civilized.

Most Centaurs were aggressive creatures, known for their wild behavior.

A Greek relief showing Oedipus and the Sphinx.

The Curse of Thebes

The people of Thebes were once terrorized by the Sphinx. This monster had a lion's body, the head of a woman, the wings of a great eagle, and a serpent-headed tail. Any traveler entering the city had to answer the beast's riddle correctly or be devoured, and many lives were lost. However, when a young man called Oedipus guessed the right answer, the enraged Sphinx threw herself off a cliff– and Thebes was at last free from its ancient curse.

THE SPHINX'S RIDDLE

What has four legs in the morning, two legs in the afternoon, and three legs in the evening?

Answer: Man – as a baby, he crawls on all fours; as an adult, he walks upright on two legs; and as an old man, he walks with the aid of a stick.

Harpies and Sirens

With the faces of women and the bodies of vultures, the Harpies swooped down from above to snatch food with their talons. The Sirens too were half bird and half woman. They sang bewitching songs to lure sailors to their deaths on jagged rocks.

The hero Odysseus encountered the Sirens on his journey back from the Trojan wars, as shown in this third-century AD mosaic.

THE CHIMERA AND PEGASUS

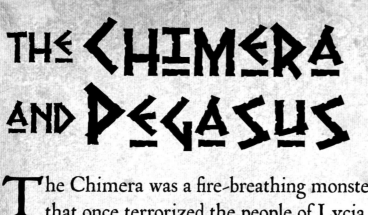

The Chimera was a fire-breathing monster that once terrorized the people of Lycia. The creature had the head and body of a fearsome lion, a goat's head arising from its back, and a deadly serpent's head at the end of its tail.

Bellerophon's Quest

At the age of 16, the hero Bellerophon set off to explore the world. However, while visiting the court of King Proteus, he angered his host–and Proteus sent him to see King Iobates in Lycia, along with a secret message that Bellerophon must be killed. Iobates longed to please Proteus, and so he challenged Bellerophon to slay the Chimera. The king was certain that like others before him, the hero would be killed by the creature's scorching breath.

Bellerophon riding the winged stallion Pegasus.

The Chimera had a serpent's head at the end of its tail.

Slaying the Beast

That same night, Athena appeared to Bellerophon. Giving him a golden bridle, she told the hero to find the winged horse Pegasus. The next day, Bellerophon came across the beautiful stallion–Pegasus reared, but Bellerophon managed to slip the bridle over his nose. As the pair flew over Lycia, Bellerophon saw the scorched land that lay around the Chimera's lair and had an idea. Guiding Pegasus back down to the ground, he found a block of lead to place on his spear, and then man and horse once again took to the skies. When the Chimera emerged from its lair, Pegasus sped down towards the beast's jaws and Bellerophon thrust his spear into its throat. The Chimera's breath melted the lead and the creature was suffocated.

SCYLLA AND CHARYBDIS

Mediterranean sailors were terrorized by a dreadful pair of monsters, Scylla and Charybdis, who lived on either side of a narrow sea channel between Italy and Sicily. Charybdis was said to lie hidden beneath a rock. Three times a day, she sucked in huge amounts of water, before spitting it out again. This created a vast, raging whirlpool that dragged ships down beneath the waves.

Gaping Jaws

Sailors desperate to avoid Charybdis risked sailing too close to the fearsome Scylla. Myth tells that this monster was once a beautiful water nymph loved by Poseidon. His wife, Amphitrite, became jealous and transformed the nymph into a beast with six long necks, each topped by a ferocious head. Concealed in her dark sea cave, Scylla silently lay in wait for passing ships. When one passed within reach, out shot her ravenous heads to snatch and devour victims.

A Greek bronze showing Scylla, the six-headed monster that terrorized Mediterranean waters.

53

In Homer's "The Odyssey", Odysseus must choose whether to confront Charybdis or Scylla.

DRAGONS AND SERPENTS

Greek myths told of many dreadful creatures with serpent and dragon-like features. Typhon, the hundred-headed serpent monster conquered by Zeus and imprisoned beneath Mount Etna, produced several fearsome offspring. Among them were the snake-tailed hound Cerberus; the fire-breathing Chimera with its serpentine tail; and the many-headed swamp dragon called the Hydra.

Heracles battles the dragon Ladon for his eleventh labor.

The serpent-like Hydra had many heads—when one was cut off, another grew back in its place.

Cadmus, the founder of Thebes, slays the dragon.

The Ismenian Dragon

Near the city of Thebes was a spring called Ismenos; it was guarded by a huge dragon sacred to Ares. When the hero Cadmus began building Thebes, he sent his men to fetch water but they were killed by the dragon's breath. Cadmus killed the beast and Athena instructed him to sow its teeth in the ground. He did as he was told, and up from the earth sprung many warriors who battled with each other until only five remained. These men helped Cadmus to build Thebes. However, Ares later took revenge for the death of the dragon, and transformed Cadmus and his wife into snakes.

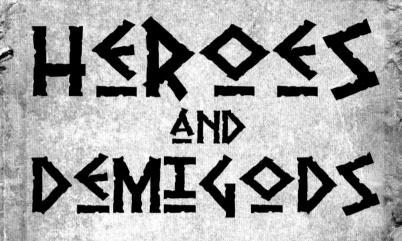

HEROES
AND
DEMIGODS

The heroes and demigods of mythical Greece performed incredible deeds and battled with dreadful monsters to prove their daring. Mighty Heracles revealed his incredible strength by carrying out superhuman feats, Jason valiantly faced the hissing dragon of the Golden Fleece, and Theseus risked all to conquer the man-eating Minotaur.

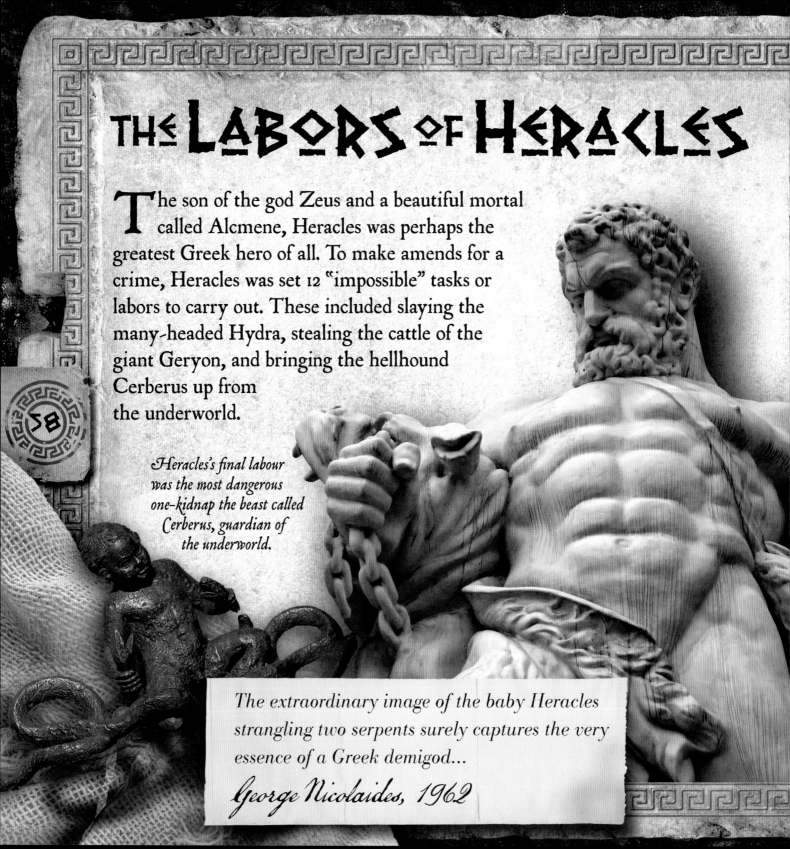

THE LABORS OF HERACLES

The son of the god Zeus and a beautiful mortal called Alcmene, Heracles was perhaps the greatest Greek hero of all. To make amends for a crime, Heracles was set 12 "impossible" tasks or labors to carry out. These included slaying the many-headed Hydra, stealing the cattle of the giant Geryon, and bringing the hellhound Cerberus up from the underworld.

Heracles's final labour was the most dangerous one—kidnap the beast called Cerberus, guardian of the underworld.

58

The extraordinary image of the baby Heracles strangling two serpents surely captures the very essence of a Greek demigod...

George Nicolaides, 1962

THE 12 LABORS OF HERACLES

1. KILLING THE NEMEAN LION
This beast had skin so thick that no weapon could pierce it. Heracles chased the lion into its cave and strangled the creature with his bare hands.

2. SLAYING THE HYDRA
When one of this serpent's many heads was sliced off, three grew back to replace it. Heracles's companion Iolaus held a flame to each wound, thus preventing the heads from growing back.

3. CAPTURING THE CERYNEIAN DEER
This golden-horned stag could run as fast as the wind. Heracles chased it for a whole year, before stopping it with an arrow fired at its front legs.

4. OBTAINING THE ERYMANTHIAN BOAR
Heracles chased this ferocious boar up Mount Erymanthus, where it became trapped in deep snow.

5. CLEANING THE STABLES OF KING AUGEAS IN ONE DAY
King Augeas had not cleaned the stable where he kept countless animals for 30 years! Heracles made two holes in the stable walls and caused two nearby rivers to sweep through the mess.

6. KILLING THE STYMPHALIAN BIRDS
These winged flesh-eaters had bronze beaks and dagger-like talons. Heracles scared them from their hiding places with a magical rattle, and shot them down one by one.

7. CAPTURING THE CRETAN BULL
Heracles wrestled this raging beast, sacred to the god Poseidon, before riding it back to King Eurystheus.

8. STEALING THE MARES OF KING DIOMEDES
Heracles overpowered the grooms of these man-eating horses before driving the beasts down to his boat.

9. FETCHING THE GIRDLE OF HIPPOLYTE
Hippolyte was the queen of the fearsome Amazon warriors. Although she initially gave Heracles her magical belt, he ended up fighting a bloody battle with the Amazons.

10. STEALING THE CATTLE OF GERYON
These magical beasts were owned by a giant with three heads and three bodies. Heracles killed Geryon with a single arrow that pierced the heart of all three bodies.

11. FETCHING THE APPLES OF HESPERIDES
The golden apples were guarded by the serpent Ladon at the very edge of the world. Atlas—who had to hold up the world as a punishment—offered to fetch the apples for Heracles. However, while he was gone, Heracles had to bear the weight of the world in his place.

12. KIDNAPPING CERBERUS, GUARDIAN OF THE UNDERWORLD
This was Heracles's most dangerous task, for very few mortals had ever descended to the land of the dead. Heracles overpowered the three-headed Cerberus with brute strength.

For his third labor, Heracles chased the Ceryneian Deer for a whole year before stopping it with an arrow.

SLAYING THE MINOTAUR

The monstrous Minotaur w[as] imprisoned in a vast maze.

The Minotaur was a horrifying monster born to the wife of King Minos of Crete. Kept at the center of a huge maze called the Labyrinth, this creature–with the body of a man and the head and tail of a bull–could only be satisfied by feasting on human flesh. Every year, 14 young people from Athens were thrown into the maze and left to their terrible fate.

Killing the Beast

The hero Theseus was determined to get rid of this ferocious creature. Ariadne, the daughter of King Minos, was in love with Theseus and gave him a ball of golden string so that he would not become lost in the maze. Wandering through the tunnels, he allowed the string to unravel behind him. Suddenly, the hero made out two eyes burning in the darkness and then the Minotaur attacked him. The two struggled for many hours until finally Theseus was victorious. By following the string, he was able to escape from the Labyrinth.

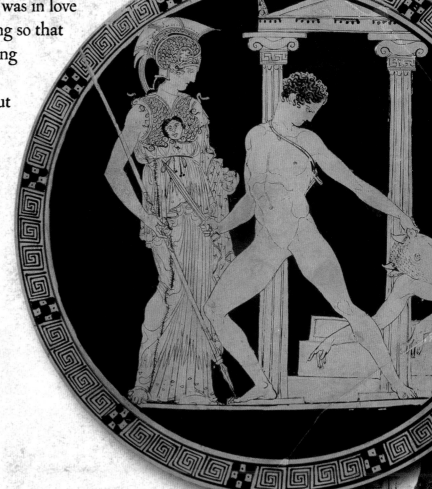

The goddess Athena with Theseus after his brave feat.

Theseus wrestles the beast to the ground before driving his sword through its throat.

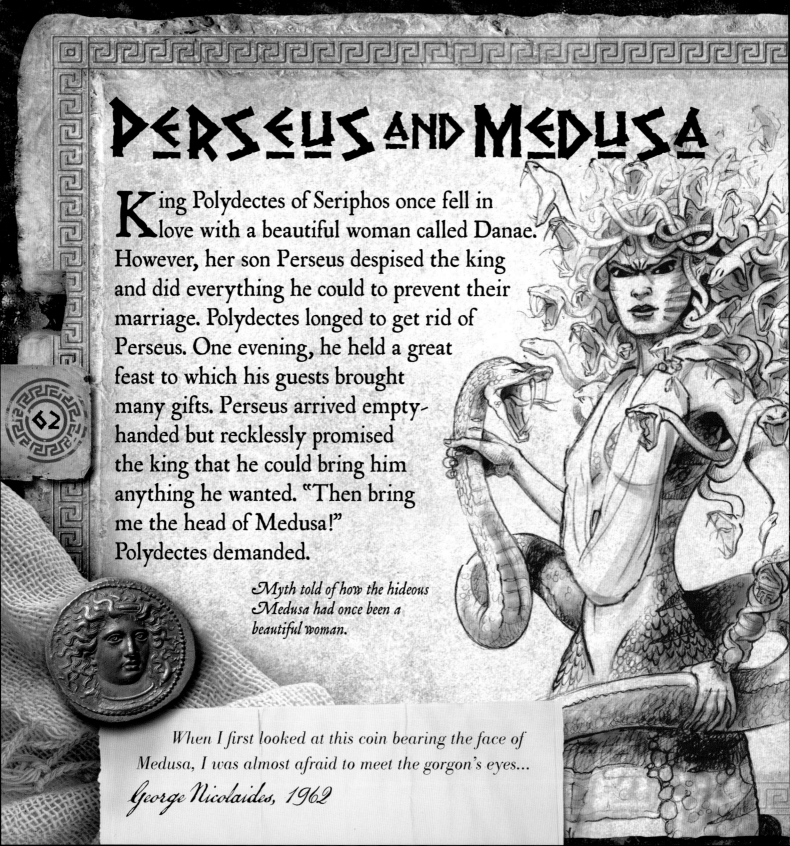

PERSEUS AND MEDUSA

King Polydectes of Seriphos once fell in love with a beautiful woman called Danae. However, her son Perseus despised the king and did everything he could to prevent their marriage. Polydectes longed to get rid of Perseus. One evening, he held a great feast to which his guests brought many gifts. Perseus arrived empty-handed but recklessly promised the king that he could bring him anything he wanted. "Then bring me the head of Medusa!" Polydectes demanded.

Myth told of how the hideous Medusa had once been a beautiful woman.

When I first looked at this coin bearing the face of Medusa, I was almost afraid to meet the gorgon's eyes...
George Nicolaides, 1962

Medusa has been portrayed by many famous artists including Gian Lorenzo Bernini (left) and Benvenuto Cellini (below).

A Deadly Gaze

The guests laughed, for no man could kill Medusa. She was one of three deadly sisters called the gorgons—a single glance at their hideous faces was enough to turn anyone to stone. Perseus prayed to the gods for help. Athena gave the young man a shield and instructed him to visit three ancient hags who could tell him where to find Medusa. Hermes gave him winged sandals, a sword and a helmet that would make him invisible. Perseus flew to the gorgons' lair—here Medusa slept, though her snaky hair writhed and hissed. As he crept closer, the gorgon awoke and turned her deadly stare upon the intruder. Perseus avoided Medusa's gaze by looking only at her reflection on his shield. Then swiftly drawing his sword, the hero sliced off the monster's head before speeding away.

Jason and the Golden Fleece

Jason was just a baby when his father, the king of Iolcos, was overthrown by his wicked brother, Pelias. Although Jason was sent far away, Pelias feared losing his power–the goddess Hera had once warned him, "beware a stranger wearing a single sandal". Aged 20, Jason decided to claim his kingdom. As he journeyed to Iolcos, he stopped to assist an old woman crossing a river. Jason entered the surging water and one of his sandals was swept away...

Jason's Quest

Pelias was horrified when his nephew appeared. He told him that he would give up the throne on one condition: Jason must fetch the Golden Fleece from the kingdom of Colchis. Pelias was sure he would never return, for the fleece was guarded by a dragon that never slept. Jason built a ship called the *Argo* then gathered together a band of heroes, the Argonauts.

Jason and the Argonauts set sail in their ship, the Argo.

The Victorious Hero

In Colchis, Jason had to carry out two tasks. The first was to yoke two fire-breathing bulls to a plough; he was protected from their breath by a magical potion. The second was to sow a field with dragons' teeth and escape the armed warriors they would grow into. He threw a rock among them, causing them to turn on each other. That night, Jason approached the tree where the fleece was hanging. Hearing the dragon's terrible hiss, the hero sprinkled a sleeping potion over the beast—as it fell asleep, he seized the fleece and carried it back to the *Argo*.

An enormous dragon guarded the Golden Fleece at all times.

THE MAGICAL RAM

The Golden Fleece had once belonged to a winged ram that helped the twins Phrixus and Helle to escape from their evil stepmother. As the ram flew over the sea to Colchis, Helle fell off and drowned. In Colchis, Phrixus sacrificed the ram to the gods and gave its fleece to King Aeëtes.

Phrixus and Helle are carried away by the golden ram.

THE WAR AGAINST TROY

Some of the most exciting tales are about Greece's war with the city of Troy. For many years, scholars believed they were no more than stories. Then, in 1870, Heinrich Schliemann discovered the site in Turkey where the ancient city of Troy had once stood. Greek myths with their accounts of heroism and treachery during the Trojan war were probably based on many different conflicts, or perhaps on a single war around the twelfth century BC.

A scene from The Iliad, Homer's epic poem set during the Trojan war.

HELEN OF TROY

Helen–considered in Greek myths to be the most beautiful woman in the world–was the wife of Menelaus, the king of Sparta. When she was stolen away by a Trojan prince called Paris, the Greeks united to besiege the city of Troy and bring Helen back to Sparta. Tales, such as *The Iliad* by the Greek poet Homer, describe the thrilling battle-exploits of warriors like the Greek hero Achilles or the Trojan hero Hektor. After 10 years, the Greeks finally tricked the Trojans into defeat.

Strong and handsome, Achilles was celebrated for his bravery in battle.

ACHILLES

As a baby, Achilles was dipped in the river Styx to make him invincible. His left heel was left unwashed, though, and he was killed by an arrow that struck it. Today, an "Achilles' heel" describes a fatal flaw in spite of overall strength.

Helen of Troy, whose beauty was legendary, was a daughter of Zeus.

THE ADVENTURES OF ODYSSEUS

After the great Trojan war, King Odysseus longed to return to his kingdom and wife, Penelope. The warrior set sail with a fleet of 12 ships, but it would be another 10 years before he finally reached Ithaca. Homer recounted the cunning hero's many extraordinary adventures in the epic poem *The Odyssey*.

Blinding the Cyclops

While exploring an island, Odysseus and his men came across a cave belonging to the Cyclops Polyphemus—who pulled a boulder across the entrance and trapped them. That night, the men drove a stake through the giant's eye. The following morning, the blinded Cyclops rolled away the stone to let his sheep out. However, the men had tied themselves beneath the sheep's bellies and escaped.

The one-eyed Polyphemus was the son of the god Poseidon.

The Enchanted Island

When Odysseus landed his ship on the golden sands of Aiaia, some of his men set about exploring. They were invited into the home of the sorceress Circe. One man, Eurylochus, was suspicious but the others were soon enjoying a delicious feast. As the men ate, Eurylochus was horrified to see them transform into grunting pigs. He raced back to tell Odysseus who set out to rescue his friends. On his way, he met the messenger god Hermes who gave him a magical herb. When Circe welcomed Odysseus with a drink, he slipped the herb into his goblet. When her guest failed to turn into a pig, Circe realized she had been outwitted. Odysseus put his sword to her throat and she quickly agreed to turn her captives back into humans.

The sorceress Circe greeted Odysseus with a golden goblet containing a magic potion.

THE HERO RETURNS

When Odysseus finally reached Ithaca, he found his house had been taken over by suitors determined to marry his wife. However, with the help of his son, Odysseus outwitted these enemies and was at last reunited with Penelope.

Odysseus with his loyal wife, Penelope.

THE TROJAN HORSE

Odysseus and the other Greek warriors hid in the hollow belly of a giant wooden horse. When the Trojans dragged the strange "gift horse" into the city, the Greeks crept from their hiding place and conquered Troy.

ACKNOWLEDGMENTS

It was my father's stirring tales that first sparked my interest in ancient Greek mythology. However, I would not have thought to write upon this subject were it not for the strange turn of events outlined in my introduction. In drawing upon that inspiration, I have been helped by many.

As well as paying tribute to my father, George Nicolaides, I would like to thank the following individuals who have made this book possible: my editor Jo Casey; Jacob da Costa and Mark Walker at Wild Pixel Ltd. for design and CGI artworks; Russell Porter for art direction; Leo Brown and Rebecca Wright for pencil artworks; Steve Behan for picture research; and Tael Steinitz for production.

Selene Nicolaides

The publishers would like to thank the following sources for their kind permission to reproduce the pictures in this book.

Key: t = top, b = bottom, c = centre, l = left & r = right

REX/Shutterstock/The Art Archive/DEA Picture Library/G. Nimatallah: 1, Istockphoto.com 2-3, Somogyvari/Getty Images 4, Getty Images/DEA/G. Dagli Orti/De Agostini 6-7t, Getty Images/CM Dixon/Print Collector 6-7b, Alamy 7b, Getty Images 8-9, Private Collection 10bl, Leemage/Corbis via Getty Images 10c, Sergio Azenha/Alamy Stock Photo 11c, Rischgitz/Getty Images 11tr, Prisma Archivo/Alamy Stock Photo 11br, Oldesign/Shutterstock.com 12c, Walters Art Museum 12b, Public Domain 16-17, Bridgeman Images/Galleria degli Uffizi, Florence 17t, Ancient Art and Architecture/ Alamy Stock Photo 17c, Bridgeman Images/Château de Versailles, France 17b, akg-images / Erich Lessing 18l, Chronicle/Alamy Stock Photo 18-19, Wead/Shutterstock.com 19tr, Mimmo Jodice 22bl, Ksenia Palimski/Shutterstock.com 23br, Bridgeman Images/Faringdon Collection, Buscot, Oxon, UK 23t, withgod/Shutterstock 26c, DEA/A. DE GREGORIO/De Agostini/Getty Images 26bl, REX/ Shutterstock/Gianni Dagli Orti 26-27, Prometheus72/Shutterstock 27br, Bridgeman Images/Louvre, Paris, France: 28bl, Istockphoto.com 28c, Bridgeman Images/Louvre, Paris, France/Peter Willi 29tr, Bridgeman Images/De Agostini Picture Library/G. Dagli Orti 30bl, Thinkstock 30b, Istockphoto. com 31t, Private Collection 31b, Alamy Stock Photo/Rex Allen 32, Istockphoto.com 32-33, Public Domain 33t, Bridgeman Images/ Louvre, Paris, France 34l, AKG-Images 34bc, Bridgeman Images/ De Agostini Library/G.Dagli Orti 35bl, The Art Collector/Print Collector/Getty Images 35r, Tatiana Popova/Shutterstock.com 36, Private Collecton 37t, akg-images/Erich Lessing 37b, Christian Baitg/ Getty Images 39, Bridgeman Images/Gift of Professor Alice Van Vechten Brown 40bl, Christian Baitg/ Getty Images 40-41, Bridgeman Images/Gallery Oldham, UK 41r, DeAgostini/Getty Images 41t, DeAgostini/Getty Images 42l & 42c, Bridgeman Images/Davis Museum and Cultural Center, Wellesley College, MA, USA/Museum purchase 42, Walters Art Museum 43l, Zde/Wikimedia Commons 43r, Bridgeman Images/© British Library Board. All Rights Reserved 44t, 44-45 Andreas Praefcke/ Wikimedia Commons, Shutterstock.com 46-47, Hulton Archive/Getty Images 48l, De Agostini/G. Nimatallah/Getty Images 48r, DEA/G. DAGLI ORTI/De Agostini/Getty Images 49b, Alamy Stock Photo/ Ancient Art & Architecture Collection Ltd 49t, Christie's Images 50bl, Bridgeman Images/ Look and Learn: 50-51, akg-images/Orsi Battaglini 51b, Bridgeman Images/Palazzo Sandi-Porto (Cipollato), Venice, Italy 51t, CM Dixon/Print Collector/Getty Images 52, Private Collection 53, Peter Horree/Alamy Stock Photo 54bl, SSPL/Getty Images 54-55, Stapleton Collection/Bridgeman Images 55tr, Mastering_Microstock/Shutterstock, Getty Images 56, Getty Images/DeAgostini 60t, Bridgeman Images/Private Collection 61l, Bridgeman Images/Museo Arqueologico Nacional, Madrid, Spain 61r, Fine Art Images/Heritage Images/Getty Images 63l, Timur Kulgarin/Shutterstock 63r, Bridgeman Images/Private Collection 65br, Danita Delimont/Getty Images 66, Bridgeman Images/Stefano Baldini 67l, Panos Karos/Shutterstock 67r, Bridgeman Images/ Museum of Fine Arts, Boston, Massachusetts, USA 68bl, DEA/G. DAGLI ORTI/De Agostini/Getty Images 69t, AKG-Images 69br

All other illustrations © Welbeck Children's Limited

Published in 2023 by Mortimer Children's

An Imprint of Welbeck Children's Limited, part of the Welbeck Publishing Group
Offices in: London - 20 Mortimer Street, London W1T 3JW
& Sydney - Level 17, 207 Kent St, Sydney NSW 2000 Australia

www.welbeckpublishing.com

Text, design and layout © Welbeck Children's Limited 2022

ISBN: 978-1-83935-264-5

Printed in Dongguan, China

10 9 8 7 6 5 4 3 2 1

FSC
www.fsc.org
MIX
Paper from responsible sources
FSC® C104723